THE LION AND THE MOUSE

A Tale of Friendship

Adapted by Sarah Toast
Illustrated by Krista Brauckmann-Towns
Other Illustrations by Marty Noble

PUBLICATIONS INTERNATIONAL, LTD.

One day, a lion was taking a nice nap in the warm sun. Nearby a busy little mouse scurried about looking for berries, but all the berries were too high for her to reach. "If only I was bigger," thought the mouse. Then the mouse spotted a lovely bunch of berries that she could reach by climbing the rock below them.

The little mouse lifted herself up onto the large rock and began picking the juicy, ripe berries. When she did, the mouse discovered that she hadn't climbed a rock at all. She had climbed right on top of the lion's head!

The lion did not like to be bothered while he was sleeping. In fact, he didn't like to be bothered at all. He awoke with a loud grumble, stood up on his paws, and looked up at the mouse. "Who dares to tickle my head while I'm taking a nap?" roared the lion.

The mouse could see how angry the lion was with her, so she jumped off his head and started to run away. The lion grabbed for the little mouse as quickly as he could, but she was too quick and he just missed her.

"Come here, little mouse!" the lion roared, as he ran after her.

The quick little mouse hurried to get away from the lion. She zigged and zagged through the grass, but the lion was always just one step behind. At last, the lion chased the mouse right back to where they had started. The poor little mouse was much too tired to run away anymore, and the lion scooped her up in his huge paw.

"Little mouse," roared the lion. "Don't you know that I am the king of the forest? Why did you wake me up from my nap by tickling my head?"

"Oh please, lion," said the mouse. "I was only trying to reach some lovely berries to eat."

"Just see how much you like it when I tickle your head," said the lion. "And wait until I wake you up from a pleasant nap you're having sometime."

"Please, lion," pleaded the mouse. "If you spare me, I am sure I will be able to help you some day."

Suddenly the lion began to smile, and then he began to laugh. "How could you, a tiny mouse, help the most powerful animal in the forest?" he chuckled. "That's so funny, I'll let you go—this time."

Then the lion laughed some more. He rolled over on his back, kicking and roaring with laughter. The mouse had to leap out of his way to avoid being crushed. Then she scurried off into the forest.

Still chuckling, the lion got up and realized he was hungry. He set out to find some lunch, and it wasn't long before he smelled food. "Oh, my!" the lion said. "What is that delicious smell?"

The lion started walking toward the good smell. Just when he thought he had found it, something horrible happened. A web of ropes fell on top of the lion!

The lion was caught in a trap set by hunters, and the more he struggled, the tighter the strong ropes held him. Fearing the hunters would soon return to the trap, the terrified lion roared for help.

The mouse heard the lion's roars from far away. At first she was a little frightened to go back, thinking the lion might want to hurt her. But the lion's cries for help made the mouse sad, and she remembered the promise she made to help him. The mouse hurried to where the lion's cries were coming from. Soon she found the lion tangled in the trap.

"Oh, lion," said the mouse. "I know what it feels like to be caught. But you don't need to worry. I'll try to help you."

"I don't think there's anything you can do," said the lion. "These ropes are very strong. I've pushed and pulled with all my might, but I can't get free."

Suddenly the mouse said, "I have an idea! Just hold still, and I'll get to work." She quickly began chewing through the thick ropes with her small, sharp teeth. She worked and worked, and before long, the mouse had chewed through enough rope for the lion to escape from the trap!

The lion wriggled his way out of the ropes. Then the lion and the mouse heard the hunters' voices as they neared the trap. "Hurry! We have to escape before they see you," said the mouse, and they ran away.

The lion was very grateful to the mouse. "I thank you for saving me, Mouse. And I am sorry that I laughed at you before," said the lion.

Then the lion scooped up the mouse and placed her on his head. He carried her back to the berry bush and lay down under it.

"Mouse," he said, "I want you to reach up and pick one of those berries that you wanted earlier today."

The mouse plucked the biggest berry she could find and tucked it under her arm. The lion took the mouse off of his head and held her in his paw. "Let's stick together," he said. "I can help you reach the berries, and you can get me out of a tight spot now and then."

"Okay!" said the mouse, and they've been friends ever since.

One to Grow On
Friendship

Friendship is a wonderful virtue. In this story, the lion and the mouse learned how to make new friends.

Sometimes, though, it's hard to be friends. At first, the lion was angry with the mouse and did not want to be friends. And the mouse was afraid because the lion was mean to her. In the end, the lion and the mouse learned that it's better to be nice than to be mean. And, although they are different, they can still be good friends.